An RRP International Publishing Breaking News Book©

# Life Lessons from a Dög Named RUDY

By Dr. Keen Babbage, Ed. D.

I0157079

INTERNATIONAL
RRP
PUBLISHING &DIGITAL MEDIA

RRP International Publishing LLC
Richmond, Ky.

RRP International LLC, DBA Eugenia Ruth LLC
330 Eastern Bypass
Ste #1 Box 302
Richmond, Ky. 40475


**www.rrpinternational.org**

ISBN-13: 978-0-9898848-8-4

# Dedication

To Rudy, an amazing dog

# Table of Contents

# Chapter 1

# Show the People You Love

# That You Love Them

Pure joy. Celebrate. Run. Wag tail. Jump. Dance. Shake. Those are parts of Rudy's enthusiastic, exuberant greeting when someone he loves enters his house.

If you have been away for an hour or a few hours, he is thrilled when you return. If you are away all day, he is even more thrilled when you return. If, due to various travel or work circumstances, it has been days or weeks since Rudy saw you, the moment you return will ignite an energetic expression of the most abundant joy and love which can be expressed by a dog.

Imagine the most vibrant cheerleading squad. They jump. They cheer. They dance. They do acrobatic demonstrations of support for their team. No cheerleading squad can match the vitality of Rudy's celebrations when someone he loves returns home.

If Rudy could hug, it would be a pick you up, spin you around, newly married couple on their honeymoon hug. For married couples, such hugs may be honeymoon and anniversary moments only. For Rudy, such expressions of joy and love occur whenever a loved one returns home, especially if the absence has been an extended one.

Rudy's expression of joy at seeing people he knows, he likes and/or he loves are not limited to the welcome home moments. Rudy eagerly interacts with people during a typical day. When you walk into the room where Rudy is, he acknowledges you, he looks up at you, he walks over to you as his wagging tail says "It is so good to see you," and then he follows you around. His cordial escort is his way of saying, "It means so much to me for us to be together."

When entering Rudy's home, after an absence of any length, his response is never, "Oh, I saw you this morning. You'll probably leave again soon. No reason for me to do anything." Similarly, his response is never, "So, you are back from that trip. You never take me. You travel and I'm here wondering when you will return. Why did you leave me for so long?"

Entering Rudy's home, after an absence of any length, initiates a celebration that matches Times Square at midnight when the old year ends and the new year begins. When people return to Rudy's home, it is for him a grand slam home run hit in the bottom of the ninth inning by the home team that was losing 5-2 and now wins in walk off style 6-5. It is the thrill of the basketball buzzer beater shot from half court that turns a 72-70 loss into a 73-72 win.

Imagine a sold out concert of 20,000 music fans at a very large indoor arena. One gentleman made elaborate arrangements through a network of friends for the performing band to dedicate a particular song to his girlfriend by name for the entire crowd to hear.

The roving camera shows the young couple on the giant screens of the arena as the song is performed. The couple exudes joy and love. As the song ends, the lead singer says, "Janet. That song was for you. From your devoted boyfriend, David. Oh. Yeah. David has something to ask you."

As the camera returns to show Janet and David, the young man proposes marriage to the young lady. She yells yes. They embrace with a hug that mutually shouts "I love you". The screens project "She Said Yes" and the band dedicates another song to the newly engaged couple.

That is how Rudy lives. Moments like the one at the concert are not once in a lifetime events for Rudy. Such moments are what make up his lifetime day to day.

Part of being Rudy is expressing love whenever he has the opportunity. He is not restricted by time factors or scheduling conflicts. His expressions of love are unrestricted. He has no reason to limit his expressions of love.

Rudy's expressions of love are G-rated, legal and ethical. He runs. He jumps. He radiates. He dances. He wags his tail. He completely directs all of his energy and attention on the person he is expressing love for.

It would be unnatural for Rudy to do any less because Rudy's nature is to love. By expressing love for people he is doing what he does best.

Rudy never tires of showing love to the people he loves. "Oh, you are back. Well, I'm having this great nap that you just interrupted, so I'm going back to sleep. We'll visit later." That is never his response to the arrival of a loved one.

"You are home! That is fantastic! I missed you! I am so glad to see you! Let's play! Let's take a walk! Let's make the most of being together now." That is his response to the arrival of a loved one. Always.

Let's ask Rudy to explain why he gets so excited and shows so much joy when his family or other favorite people arrive at his house. "Are you kidding? I love these people. I really, really love them. They mean everything to me. Seeing them is the best part of each day. What could be better than seeing the people I love? I can't help myself. I love these people and I'm always going to be sure they know that. Oh, yeah. One more thing. I would never deny myself the chance to show the people I love that I love them. I can't keep my love for them stuffed inside me. Do you understand what I mean?"

Understanding what Rudy means about expressing love is one of the life lessons Rudy teaches by his excellent example. He is always in love gear. Consider this: I arrive in my car on the block of the street where Rudy and his family live. It is late afternoon on a weekday. I was at the school where I teach from about 7:00 a.m. through 5:30 p.m. today. I will take Rudy for a walk before I go home to grade papers.

By the time my car pulls up to Rudy's house, he is already at the front door celebrating our upcoming visit, our walk, and the treat he will get after we walk. How did he know to be at the door? Did he hear my car? Does he have an internal clock that tells him when it is late afternoon which is when I usually can visit with him? Let's ask Rudy.

"I can hear cars. They sound different. Some cars make sounds that tell me it will be only a few seconds before my family is home. I like that advance notice so I can be 100% ready to welcome them. Plus, I'm optimistic. I always hope that cars on our street are bringing my family. If a car comes and it's not my family, I can still feel good that it is some other dog's family and they will be happy soon."

For Rudy, it apparently requires no thinking, planning or decision making to show love to the people he loves. He made the love decision over 13 years ago when he joined this family. It has been non-stop love for those 13 years, one celebration at a time, thousands of celebrations during that time.

Showing love for the people he loves is part of being Rudy. There is a vital life lesson. Make showing love for the people you love part of who you are. Rudy never misses an opportunity to express love. Great example, Rudy.

Rudy also reminds us why. Everyone benefits. It is meaningful, joyous and pleasing for Rudy when he expresses love. As he runs, dances, jumps, wags his tail to express his love, those actions themselves are pleasant for Rudy and pleasant for the person receiving Rudy's expression of love. Rudy knows to not limit, withhold or stop something that is wholesome, proper and good if it is beneficial to everyone involved, including him.

Rudy shows the people he loves that he loves them. He does that very often. Love should be that way.

Life Lesson Notes For The Reader:

Ways to apply Life Lesson 1–*Show the People You Love That You Love Them*:

In my life:

With family:

With friends:

At work or at school:

With other people or in other places:

# Chapter 2

# Appreciate the Wonder of

# Creation

1,000 walks or more. The same path each time. About 15 minutes per walk. Rudy is always ready to take a walk. When I arrive at his house he celebrates my arrival, jumps for joy, dances for delight, runs for rejoicing and goes to the laundry room where his leash is on a shelf. Then he goes to the door clearly communicating, "It's time right now. Let's walk. Please get the leash and let's go explore everything."

He's right. Walk, walk more, keep walking. Whenever a

walk can be experienced, take a walk. For Rudy, walks are not about steps taken, dog business done or exercise, although all of that happens. Walks are all about being outside together, smelling everything that has any aroma, noticing every part of nature that is encountered and fully appreciating the endless wonder of creation.

How does he accomplish all of that on what otherwise looks like nothing more than a regular walk? That's the point. Rudy makes anything regular into something amazing. What is his method for transforming the regular into the amazing?

When we walk, he thoroughly interacts with what might seem commonplace. That interaction creates something amazing out of what otherwise would be latent or inert.

A tree can be noticed, sniffed and walked around. Far better to do all of that than to efficiently and quickly march past the tree as if the tree did not exist. The tree does exist. Rudy notices the tree. Rudy investigates the tree. Rudy smells the tree. Rudy finds the tree to be interesting. Rudy appreciates the tree's contribution to nature, to the neighborhood, to the path of the walk.

A tree that, if I were alone, I would rapidly walk past barely noticing or not noticing at all, captivates Rudy. I would be inclined to think, it's a tree. Rudy acts so he can communicate, "Look! It's a tree! It smells so good! It has all of those new buds on it as spring begins to renew the tree! It is not the same as it was yesterday! It's growing! That is so wonderful!"

It would be easy to say that since Rudy does not have a job or a daily to-do list of tasks and chores, that certainly he has the time and can move at a relaxed pace to fully observe a tree.

Rudy does have a job. His job is to fully live so the complete dogness that is within him is expressed, is developed, is applied every day. One of the impressive parts of Rudy's vast dogness is his ability to fully and to always appreciate the wonder of creation.

As I write this page in April 2013, Rudy and I just returned from a walk. We took the same path as we did on two earlier walks today. That is the same path we have taken for 13 years. It is the same path we have used for 1,000 or more walks, yet this afternoon is the first and only time for us to take that one particular walk.

Rudy makes each walk unique. When Rudy is asked, "Would you like to take a walk?" I put some enthusiastic, energetic emphasis on the word walk. He responds with a light in his eyes, with a wag of his tail, with a run to the door and he is saying, "Yes! Yes! Yes! Thank you!"

He never communicates "Oh, if we have to. I guess. But let's get it over with soon." He never expresses, "Another walk. Is it really necessary? And we'll go where we always go. It's so boring. Aren't you tired of doing this over and over?"

His response is always a vibrant "Yes!" to the opportunity to walk. I understand that as an equally vibrant "Yes!" to life itself. If there is one more walk to take, then take the walk. If there is a tree to appreciate anew, take the walk so the tree can be appreciated. If there is family member or friend who will go on a walk with you, then go. It's not just about the walk. It's about walking together, being together, sharing time together.

Rudy's perspective on walks and Rudy's full delight in walks reveal the importance of another life lesson: appreciate the wonder of creation. That life lesson has three powerful words in it separated by an article and a preposition. Appreciate. Wonder. Creation.

A tree cannot be appreciated when it is not noticed. Another person cannot be appreciated when he or she is not noticed. A tree is a complex, intriguing (intreeguing!), majestic part of creation that once was a tiny seed or plant or sapling. It has grown into so much more than it once was. It changes during the year as it reflects the seasons. It can provide shade or fruit or benefits to the atmosphere. On a closer look, there is much to appreciate about a tree. Rudy takes those closer looks at trees, at people, at all of creation.

To wonder is to think with a creative vitality. To see something or someone as a wonder is to really notice the actual or the potential goodness of what they are or who they are, what they can become, who they can become. Rudy looks, smells and touches creation to probe into its wonder. He goes beyond the initial appearance or the superficial into the intricate detail and design. He gets much out of life by fully realizing the wondrous creation of all life, but not only quantity, rather the quality. There is much to appreciate in the wonder of one walk, in one tree, of one person. Rudy does that.

Appreciating the wonder of creation is emphasized by Rudy on each walk with his specific attention to the details of creation.

Sure, Rudy notices some mailboxes, a fire hydrant or a loud car, but they get minimal attention. People, dogs, trees, grass, plants, bushes, flowers, the wind, rain, snow–he loves to romp in snow–transcend everything that is built, constructed or manufactured in getting Rudy's attention and appreciation. He concentrates on what has been created knowing that those parts of life have immensely more worth and value and meaning. He is right.

The thoughts on appreciating the wonder of creation will conclude with an idea about the creator, God.

Consider these conversations. God says to a person who is walking to his parked car in hope of beating traffic going to work on a hurried Monday morning. "Good morning, Thomas. Before you go to work I'd like to ask what you think of that tree. The one close to where your car is parked. It is showing signs of new growth this spring."

Thomas quickly replies, "It's a great tree. A really great tree. I'm sorry I have to go so fast. Let's talk more later."

God says to Rudy, "Good morning, Rudy. Now that you've had a walk, I wondered what you thought of that tree you just looked at so closely."

"It is an amazing tree. It is one of my favorites. It smells so good, especially now in spring. It looks beautiful. You did fantastic work when you made that tree. I can't wait to go look at it again. Please tell me all about the tree."

Imaginary conversations? Yes. Real life lessons to be learned? Yes, Amen.

Life Lesson Notes For The Reader:

Ways to apply Life Lesson 2–*Appreciate the Wonder of Creation*:


In my life:


With family:

With friends:

At work or at school:

With other people or in other places:

# Chapter 3

# Naps are Good

Infants take many naps. Toddlers take some naps. Young children take a few naps. Senior citizens take naps. For the age groups in between, naps are often in the unlikely category. Do naps become bad when a person becomes 13 years old and stay bad until the person retires five or six decades later? No. Naps are good. Just ask Rudy about naps.

"I really like naps. A good day for me includes one or two long naps in the morning. Then more naps in the afternoon. Of course, I will gladly end a nap or postpone a nap if someone offers to take me for a walk or when someone arrives at home and I get to celebrate their return. But on most days I can count on four good naps, maybe five. Naps are good. More naps are better."

Not all naps are alike. Rudy has many places where he very comfortably takes a nap. The most serious naps, the naps that are intended to last an hour or two, are on the sofa in the television room. Rudy has no interest in television, but he can seriously sleep on the couch in the television room.

He gives himself two options on the sofa. First, he could rearrange the pillows and get on top of them so his head can relax on one of the sofa's arm rests. Second, he can get exactly in the middle of the sofa where the two large cushions meet. That slight valley between those cushions seems to be a perfect place to snuggle with the sofa.

What causes him to select the first option or the second option on the sofa? There is a pattern. If he is with someone who is in the room, he prefers the middle. If he is alone, he prefers to sleep atop the pillows. Perhaps the pillows give him some company and he thinks of them as toys or as friends.

He clearly plans the sofa naps. It requires a big leap to get on the sofa. He can make the leap, but it takes some effort and preparation. He looks like a track sprinter getting his or her feet set in the starting blocks prior to an initial burst of speed to begin a race. He measures the jump. He sets his feet. He rocks back and forth. Then, he boldly, confidently and successfully lands on the sofa. He seems to be very pleased with this achievement. He knows it will be followed by a long, luxurious nap.

There are other times when the floor is the desired place for a nap. He knows that the sofa is always available, but the sofa is not always selected.

There are some chairs he likes to sleep under. Perhaps they provide a fort for him. There are some walls he likes to sleep against. Perhaps they provide a partial hug. There are some carpeted areas that sometimes he will select, but not very often. The room with the best carpet is where he likes to keep his toys so he must associate that room with play instead of naps.

There are a few chairs that he will jump into occasionally for a nap, but he seems to prefer a chair if someone is sitting there and he can join them not for a nap, but for a visit. He seems to categorize chairs as good places to visit with someone more than as places for a solitary nap.

In addition to a system of selecting the right location for each nap, Rudy has given himself options for how to lie down during a nap. For the shorter naps, he is in the Sphinx position except his head will rest in front between his paws or just off to one side. For the super long naps when he is really tired, Rudy is on his side with all four legs extended outward.

What makes naps so good for Rudy? What makes naps so good for anyone, dog or human? Rudy listens to his body. When his body tells him that it is time to take a nap, he does not argue or resist. He takes a nap. Of course, he has the advantages of not having a job to go to daily, nor does he have chores to do at home or errands to run. He has a nap-friendly schedule.

What advice could Rudy give about helping people fit naps into their schedules? Ask him. "That's easy. Turn off the television and take a nap. Why do people watch that screen? When I am awake I watch people or what I can see outside through a window. Just turn off the television and take a nap instead. A good nap is better than any television program."

Despite several naps each day, Rudy sleeps effortlessly through each night for eight or nine hours. He awakens each morning when people wake him up. How do the naps not interfere with sleeping well at night? Ask Rudy.

"When I lie down to sleep I lie down to sleep. I do not think about problems like when will I get to take my next walk. Of course, I can't really think, but there are images in my memory. I just concentrate fully on one thing at a time. Naptime gets my full attention. Later, playing will get my full attention. Then a walk will get my full attention. I do one thing at a time with total concentration on that one thing. It makes me a better napper, player and walker."

Admittedly, Rudy cannot use his leisure time to read a book or work on a hobby. Naps are one of his favorite uses of free time because there are times when there is nothing else to do. But in those times he could pace the floor or sit and whine. No, he takes a nap. He has options. He decides on the nap option. Smart dog. Naps are good.

As I write this page Rudy is absolutely completely involved with a nap. He is seriously asleep. He is perfectly tranquil. He is fully relaxed. He is totally peaceful.

If I woke him up with the words, "Rudy boy, would you like to take a walk?" he would quickly sit up and get excited. "Did someone say walk? Great. Let's walk right now. Thank you so much." He would not say, "Maybe later. I really need to finish this nap." The nap will finish as soon as the walk offer is made.

Naps are good, but naps can't equal a walk. Rudy has very proper priorities. Take a long, restful, soothing nap alone. That is good. Take a great walk with a beloved family member so we can appreciate the wonder of creation anew. That is even better.

The best day would include naps and walks. Rudy knows that the ideal is not one or the other; rather, the ideal is both. Today will be a day of several naps and several walks. Naps are good. Walks are great. Both are better. Do both. That's the ideal.

Life Lesson Notes For The Reader:

Ways to apply Life Lesson 3–*Naps are Good*:


In my life:


With family:


With friends:


At work or at school:


With other people or in other places:

# Chapter 4

# Play, Play More, Keep Playing

There is play and there is RUDY PLAY. The difference is energy, vitality, enthusiasm, joy and delight.

For Rudy's favorite play activity, the only item needed is a towel. The floor of the cage box structure which he gladly, securely and comfortably sleeps in at night has two bath towels on it. He can arrange these two towels as bedding according to his preferences on any given night.

The towel game comes in the morning, in the afternoon and/or in the evening. Rudy decides when. It begins as he walks very purposefully to the cage box and uses his nose to open the door. Then he uses his mouth and a paw to pull one towel out of the cage box. He is always very pleased with himself when he successfully removes a towel from the cage box.

Then he issues a challenge as he looks up and clearly communicates, "This is my towel. Just try to take it away from me." Rudy is a very gentle and friendly dog, but wear gloves when you play the towel game with him because the same canine teeth which are determined to help maintain possession of the towel could unintentionally scrape a finger.

Rudy's rule in the towel game is that possession equals victory. His determined approach to keeping possession is to get part of the towel in front of him, part of the towel in his mouth locked in a powerful grip and all of the rest of the towel under him. For Rudy, the towel game is a total body experience.

The challenger tries to pull any part of the towel away from Rudy. Rudy's reactions are quite quick and his will to win is endless.

There are times when he shifts positions and will get a tight grip with his mouth on the towel. He then shakes his head and neck intensely from side to side as if he must conquer the towel itself.

He adds sound effects. The growling sound Rudy makes during the towel game is made at no other time or for no other reason. This game has a ritual, a ceremony which Rudy created and perfected. It is his game. It is his towel. Yet he cannot play the towel game alone.

Rudy plays the towel game not to control the towel or to defeat the challenger, but to interact. The towel is a prop. The joy is in playing the game with someone. Rudy understands that the best part of play is the activity with someone. Sure, he likes the towel, he likes the tug-of-war pulling on the towel as the challenger tries to take the towel, and he likes making the sound effects which are unique to this competition. He dearly enjoys all of that.

But he loves the fact that someone cared enough to play with him. It is as if he is saying, "This game lets me know that you are still here with me and that you really like me. When you play with me it tells me that I really matter to you."

It is said that children spell love t-i-m-e. Rudy often uses the same thinking and the same spelling. It's not primarily about the play itself although that is desired. It's more about the time together. Increase the play and you increased the time shared together, the memories created together, the smiles and laughs expressed together. Thanks, Rudy, for that good life lesson.

Rudy's eagerness to play is one manifestation of his love for life. Rudy loves being alive. Rudy loves living.

For example, two or three members of Rudy's family are sitting in the kitchen talking. Rudy is with them, but then he leaves the room. He returns soon and shows everyone that he has a rubber ball in his mouth. The ball is not for display purposes–it is for play.

Rudy could play with the ball by himself. He can roll it on the floor and fling it through the air. But he did not bring the ball into the kitchen to demonstrate his rolling and flinging skills. He brought the ball to offer an invitation to play.

Now, if he could play with the ball alone, why is he seeking someone who will play with him? For Rudy, play is not about the ball. Play is about the interaction with the people who play with you. Rudy is seeking to add joy, energy, pleasure and interaction to life. For Rudy, the togetherness part of playing together is the best part.

When Rudy brings the ball to me I always stop what I am doing and start playing. I can get back to my other tasks or duties soon. Rudy is reminding me to put the most into life and to get the most out of life.

We will play for about five minutes and Rudy will be quite ready to lie down, but even that is interactive. He will lie down on the floor very close to the chair where I am sitting. He will be quiet and still, but also interactive if in no other way than to say there is no other place I'd rather be than with you where you are.

Play is active togetherness. Rudy puts much activity into his life, into the life of his family. He fully lives. Play is part of that fullness of life for Rudy. Throughout each day of his life, Rudy fully lives. When he plays, it is with total concentration, complete effort and pure joy. It is one of his many ways to fully live. How very wise he is.

Rudy never communicates "I know we played with the ball yesterday, but we might as well do that again today." Rather he communicates, "Look what we get to do now! We get to play with the ball. Isn't that great? It will be so good to do this together. What could be better for us right now?"

Rudy lives now. Rudy lives fully right now. Rudy lives fully in every now. Smart dog, very smart dog.

Life Lesson Notes For The Reader:

Ways to apply Life Lesson 4–*Play, Play More, Keep Playing*:

In my life:

With family:

With friends:

At work or at school:

With other people or in other places:

# Chapter 5

# Ask Politely for What You

# Would Like to Have

My mother liked Rudy a lot. Rudy certainly like her. He was especially glad to see her when the family gathered to celebrate Christmas, Thanksgiving, a birthday or any other occasion that included serving food.

My mother, known as Nana to her grandchildren, loved being with members of the family. She told my brother and me that her goal in life was to be a good mother. She surpassed that goal. She reached perfection as a mother.

At family celebrations when cake and ice cream were served, Nana enthusiastically consumed both. Due to health issues, sweets were off limits for Nana, but we made exceptions occasionally.

Nana was most likely to make exceptions for Rudy. Dogs need to avoid desserts, but Nana always gave Rudy a bite of cake. When we told her not to do that she said sincerely, "You tell him to stop looking at me like that." Rudy's most effective look would continue and for all of Nana's life would get results.

At family gatherings when food is served, Rudy optimistically sits on the floor near the table. He looks up with eyes full of hope, ears full of eager anticipation of the sound of a bite hitting the floor and a heart full of love when he sees an outstretched hand offering him a table treat.

Of course, much food for people is not intended for dogs. Rudy does not know that. He likes to be involved in everything his family does and that includes meals.

Rudy has a variety of methods he uses when appealing for food. He will sit sometimes at a perfect 45 degree angle as his head, back and tail are arranged with geometric perfection. He looks attentively, eagerly, hopefully and with total concentration at the person who is preparing food or is seated to eat food. He just makes his presence known and if he can catch your eye he will win because his perfected look instantly convinces anyone that Rudy deserves a taste of the food he is so vibrantly smelling.

There are times when Rudy is more subtle. Someone is preparing any type of food in the kitchen and Rudy lies on the floor with his head elevated slightly. He is ready to sprint toward any piece of food which happens to reach the floor. The floor in the kitchen never needs to be swept for dropped food when Rudy is involved.

Then there is Rudy's most determined effort which involves sounds. As he has grown older his vocabulary has increased. There are specific sounds he makes to express degrees of eagerness to get a taste of food. The sounds never include a bark or a growl. The sounds are on a scale from whine, to whimper, to negotiate, to plead, to implore, to convince.

He is patient, but persistent. He is polite and hopeful. He is cordial and confident. He is determined to convince people that they will experience much joy by providing him with a tiny portion of the food they are eating.

Food is not Rudy's only objective of his mannerly efforts. When he goes to a door and sits, but does not move, it is a clear request for him to go outside. If he is not taken out soon, he will look at the first person he sees and then look again at the door. He is sending a clear message "Would you please take me outdoors for a walk?"

One of Rudy's favorite treats is a specialty dog food which to him is the ultimate dining delight. Small bags of this exotic delicacy are kept on a shelf high above his water bowl and his regular food bowl. The regular food bowl always has tasty supplies of very healthy, very crunchy dog food, so he is able to dine at any time; however, the delicacy treat is given to him in limited amounts for certain reasons.

Rudy likes to walk into the laundry room where his water and food bowls are and look up at the shelf where he knows the delicacy is stored. He is asking politely for a treat. His approach works often enough for him to keep trying.

Rudy's ears itch occasionally. He does all he can to relieve this by aligning himself with the edge of an area rug and sliding himself along that edge so the carpet scratches him. Another option is to vigorously rub himself–it looks as if he is practicing a swimming stroke–against a carpeted area where the floor in one room drops down about six inches to create a step into an adjacent room. That six-inch ledge works as a self-scratching system for Rudy.

Rudy reduces or stops his efforts with the carpet or the carpeted ledge whenever someone comes to him and starts scratching his ears. His individual effort is partly an attempt to stop the itching, but is also a polite request for a family member to help him solve the itching problem.

There are times when the person who is walking Rudy will stop to speak with a neighbor. Rudy has learned to calmly, patiently and politely sit and wait for the conversation to end. Then it is time for the adventure of walking to begin anew. He seems to realize that his patient, polite waiting can earn a longer walk and a larger post-walk treat. Rudy knows that there are many reasons to be polite.

Rudy does not get everything that he politely asks for, but his manners are consistent. He must realize that he will get nothing if he is rude, yet he could get something if he is polite. He may also realize that being polite is just right. Being polite is another way for Rudy to express love.

Life Lesson Notes For The Reader:

Ways to apply Life Lesson 5–*Ask Politely for What You Would Like to Have*:

In my life:

With family:

With friends:

At work or at school:

With other people or in other places:

# Chapter 6

# Respond Lovingly to the

# Needs of Others

During October 2010 through January 2011, I was treated for Stage 4 sinus cancer. The care required to fight that disease and to endure the brutal radiation/chemotherapy treatments, meant that I spent many days and nights at the home of my brother, Bob, and sister-in-law, Laura. Of course, that is also Rudy's home.

During those very difficult months my energy level was often near zero. I took many naps. When not napping, I was often motionless on a sofa or in a reclining chair. Rudy knew that something was different because Uncle Keen never spent the night before.

Rudy also sensed that something was wrong. His eagerness to be together with his family altered into also becoming my guardian, my watchdog, my constant companion. When all I could do was lie down on a reclining chair, Rudy was content to lie down next to that chair. If I moved, he would look up to be sure that all was well.

For some reason, I was most comfortable sleeping on a couch in the living room. At bedtime, I would stretch out on the long couch and cover up for warmth. Then Rudy would jump up onto the couch and settle in at the end of the couch where there was just enough room between my feet and the armrest.

Rudy has several other places in the house where he likes to sleep overnight; in truth, they are places where he prefers to sleep overnight including his cage box. Still, during those times while I was being treated for cancer that I spent nights at Rudy's house, he sacrificed sleeping in some of his favorite places to instead keep watch over me.

Rudy did not have to do that, but, in another sense, yes he did. Being Rudy means responding lovingly to the needs of others. How would Rudy explain this?

"Uncle Keen visits often, but he never spends the night. Now he is spending a lot of nights. I don't know the reason, but I do know that if he is here overnight, something might be wrong and he needs my help. When I am sick, I need people to take care of me. So, if Keen is sick, he needs me to help take care of him."

Rudy would never ignore the fact that I was spending the night at his house. He responded to that fact in pure Rudy style. He showed his concern. He actively expressed his concern. He gave up his preference and comfort to increase the comfort of someone else. That is just part of being Rudy. He never considered any other option.

In March 2013, my sister-in-law was out of town for several days. She returned home late on a Sunday night. Rudy was already asleep for the night, but he woke up and celebrated when Laura returned.

On Monday morning when Rudy woke up and was let out of

the overnight cage he really likes to sleep in, he ran upstairs to say "Good Morning" to Laura. He occasionally goes upstairs, but certainly a sprint up the stairs is not how he begins his days usually. On this Monday there was no other way to begin the day. How would Rudy explain that?

"My mother is home. She was gone for several days or more. Now she is home. As soon as I woke up and was let out of the cage box I remembered that she is home. How could I just wait for her to come downstairs? I had to welcome her home again. The only way to start this day is to show her how happy I am that she is home."

Rudy understands that responding lovingly to the needs of others requires being there, but is not a requirement that limits him from doing something else. Rather, it is an opportunity to be the dog he is meant to be.

As I write this chapter, I am sitting at the kitchen table in Rudy's home. Rudy has the free choice to be anywhere in the house. He likes the basement because sometimes he finds a bite of food left from a social gathering the day before. He enjoys the upstairs because there is one bathroom which has a small area rug that is extra plush and comfortable. He spends most of his time on the first floor level because that is where most of his favorite places and things are.

At this moment, Rudy is peacefully sleeping a few feet away from me. Why? "That's easy. If Uncle Keen is in the kitchen then the best place to be is in the kitchen. Why be anywhere else? It's where I can be with people I care about."

To respond most lovingly to the needs of others involves being with those other people. Rudy reminds us that we make an extra effort when something is most important. It is another part of being the best Rudy he can be.

Rudy is an especially aware dog. He hears every sound. He notices every movement. He watches every action. He smells absolutely every scent. He notices, absorbs and interacts with the fullness of life.

Rudy's total awareness is matched with a fully developed sensitivity. He cares about, he is interested in, he seeks to interact with all he hears, all he watches, all he sees, all he smells.

Whenever possible, Rudy responds to that which he is aware

of and sensitive to. Awareness, sensitivity and responses form a three-part sequence which guides Rudy moment-to-moment, day-to-day. It is part of how he vibrantly lives: fully involved, fully active, fully fascinated, fully impacting all he can to do the most to enhance life for others and for himself.

Rudy fully lives. Responding lovingly to the needs of others is an essential aspect of fully living.

Life Lesson Notes For The Reader:

Ways to apply Life Lesson 6–*Respond Lovingly to the Needs of Others*:

In my life:

With family:

With friends:

At work or at school:

With other people or in other places:

# Chapter 7

# Actions Matter

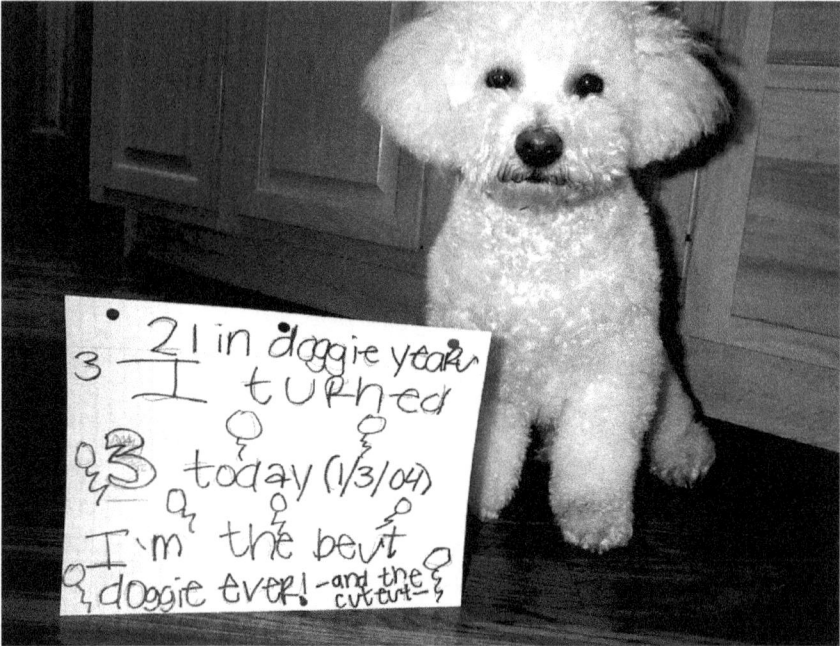

For Rudy, life is not a concept to be pondered philosophically. For Rudy, life is at its best when it is vibrantly, actively, abundantly, eagerly lived.

Rudy has endured difficulties. For many years he has been likely to have allergic skin reactions which are commonly called "hot spots." These irritate him, annoy him and cause pain. He is inclined to lick these areas or to scratch these areas, but those responses can make the condition worse.

Allergy medicine can help, although he is not eager to have a pill manipulated in his mouth and throat so he swallows it. The hot spot condition on his tail got so bad once that he had to wear a head/neck cone to minimize his effort to lick and to unknowingly aggravate the condition.

Rudy also had to make the adjustments when the children in our family—my nephews, Robert and Brian, plus my niece, Julie—went away to school. Rudy's first several years with the family included having five wonderful people at home. That provided frequent interaction and on some days there was constant interaction.

When Robert is home from his career or when Julie and Brian are home from college, Rudy smiles, rejoices, showers love on them and affirms the goodness of his life. He never lets the fact that he misses them when they are gone keep him from the full actions of expressing his joy when they return.

Despite the occasional skin hot spots, Rudy has had superior health during his 13 years of very active living. He inherently, innately, instinctively knows what actions will enhance his health, his fitness and his life. Actions matter and Rudy consistently takes the right actions.

Rudy's program for good health includes the following actions: take walks, take naps, eat the proper food almost always, drink water, play, love and get a good night's sleep. How does Rudy know to do all of that? He is one smart dog.

Rudy and I were walking one Sunday afternoon about 3:30. My sister-in-law, Laura and my brother, Bob, had been out of town overnight. They were due back at home about 4:00 on this Sunday afternoon.

While Rudy and I were walking, Bob and Laura were driving along the street very close to their home. Rudy noticed their car, heard their voices and sprinted home. No other action was possible. We were no longer merely on a walk. We were in the first moments of a joyous reunion to celebrate and be excited about.

It was obvious that Rudy did not react this way: "Oh, they're back, but eventually they will leave again. I'll just keep walking and see them in a few minutes. They aren't stopping for me so why should I run to them."

It was obvious, instead, that Rudy did react this way: "My mother and father are home. This is great. Hurry. Hurry. Hurry. The faster I get home, the sooner I can see my family." He took the action that was most genuine, most sincere, most thoughtful, most kind, most caring, most loving, most Rudy.

There have been many weekends during my years as a high

school teacher when I had 10 or 15 hours of papers to grade. On some of those Saturdays, I would take stacks of papers with me to Rudy's house. The papers would get graded. That work was always done more efficiently and more productively when I was at Rudy's home than when I was alone at my residence. Rudy explains, "Keen, you have so much work to do. Bring the work to my house. Then you can take a break occasionally and we can take walks. Everyone wins."

He is right. It is not that my amount of work is less, but having some company while I work is encouraging. The walks are invigorating and it is walks, plural, if I stay for many hours. Actions matter. Give Rudy and me eight hours and that equals three or four walks.

I get ten hours of school work done in eight hours. Rudy gets several walks to punctuate the hours of naps he is taking. The day is better for both of us. Anything that needs to be done at the house is taken care of. Rudy is right. Everyone wins when the right actions are taken in the right ways for the right reasons.

When visitors, guests or friends come to Rudy's house, he gets up and welcomes them. Actions matter. Rudy acknowledges the presence of someone who has made the effort to visit his home, his family or him. The visitor probably did not come to see Rudy, but the visitor is going to be welcomed by Rudy as an expression of his canine hospitality and delight to see them.

Rudy could continue his nap when a visitor arrives. Rudy could remain in his comfortable, relaxed position on the sofa when a guest enters his home. Not Rudy. He makes the effort and he takes the action to show how welcome the person is. Rudy is not a spectator of the moment-to-moment events and occasions at his home. Rudy is actively involved in life at his home. Rudy absorbs that life, thrives on that life and adds much more to that life than can be measured.

Why not take one more walk together, today, right now? That is Rudy's hope, suggestion and question. What else could be done in the next 15 minutes that cannot wait until after a walk? The action of and the interaction of a walk are uniquely available only if we take the walk. Actions matter. Everyone in favor of taking a walk right now, let's go. Everyone else, you need to follow our example. This moment, this action, this walk is a gift we can give ourselves. Why reject such a valuable gift?

Life Lesson Notes For The Reader:

Ways to apply Life Lesson 7–*Actions Matter*:

In my life:

With family:

With friends:

At work or at school:

With other people or in other places:

# Chapter 8

# Always Hope, Always Believe

About 4:00 p.m. each afternoon Rudy moves to the front hall of his home. He looks out the window which is vertically parallel to the front door. Then he sits along one step on the stairway which is just across from the front door. From this comfortable perch, Rudy can see events as they unfold in his front yard, on the street near his home and in the street area directly in front of his home.

I have never seen this late afternoon sequence because I am at school where I work. The school days begin for me about 7:00 a.m. and usually finish about 5:00 or 5:30 p.m. Whenever possible, I stop by Rudy's house after I leave school so we can take a walk after I visit with whoever is at home.

Rudy has acquired a sense of time. He knows when it is late afternoon. He knows when it is the time of day when I am most likely to arrive. He always hopes, always believes that there will be a late afternoon visit. It often happens, but when it does not Rudy continues to hope and continues to believe that it will happen at about 4:00 p.m. on the next day.

Each time when these afternoon visits end and I go to my car to head home, Rudy stands at the front door area looking out the adjacent window. To the extent that a dog can "think," I often wonder what Rudy is "thinking" as I enter my car and he sees me leave. Rudy can tell us.

"Oh, that is easy to explain. As I stand at the window and watch, I am saying thank you and please return soon. Watching you leave is not sad for me because I am so glad that you came today and I am certain that you will return soon, tomorrow I hope. I always hope and I always believe that whenever my family members leave they will return soon. It has always worked that way. I hope and I believe it will always work like that."

Rudy's willingness to always hope and to always believe has a firm foundation. His water bowl is never empty. His food bowl is never empty. He gets to go outside every day. He gets to take a walk or walks almost every day.

Hope and belief for Rudy are also based on his emphasis on what he has rather than what he does not have. He does not see himself with a family that sometimes has to leave. He knows he has a family that always comes back to be with him. He does not have a water bowl or a food bowl that are getting low on supplies. He has a water bowl and a food bowl that are always replenished.

He does not look at his toys that sit idly and become discouraged because there is no playing occurring. He runs to a toy, brings it to show a person and invites you to play. The invitation is always accepted. He hoped it would be accepted. He believed it would be accepted. In truth, life has taught him to know that it will be accepted.

Rudy knows that hope and faith are good. He so often sees what he hopes for happen. He so often has the experience of what he believed would happen actually occuring.

There are days when he hopes that I will arrive to take him for a walk, but I do not come on that day. He continues to hope again the next day.

There are times when he believes that a family member will give him a bite to eat during the family meal, but he ends up with nothing. He continues to believe again at the next meal.

Rudy must know what hope adds to his life. He must also realize what believing adds to his life. For Rudy, a day well lived is more than a collection of separate events, activities and encounters. For Rudy, each day brings some or much of what he hopes for and what he believes in. He does not get everything he wants, but a life of hope and a life of belief surpass a life of despair.

Rudy hopes always. Rudy believes always. Those characteristics are part of who Rudy is, how Rudy lives and the attitude that Rudy has about life.

Rudy's family members individually and collectively have given him reasons to have this attitude. What Rudy hopes for and believes in actually happen often enough to sustain his hopefulness and his faith.

What a wonderful treasure to have been given. What a blessing indeed to be the people who can convince Rudy that his hopes and his beliefs are valid because those people so often make them come true.

Rudy always hopes. Rudy always believes. He is not alone in his hopes and his beliefs. He shares his hopes and his beliefs. Hopes and beliefs shared are more likely to be implemented and manifested than those which remain isolated and hidden.

Life Lesson Notes For The Reader:

Ways to apply Life Lesson 8–*Always Hope, Always Believe*:


In my life:


With family:


With friends:

At work or at school:

With other people or in other places:

# Chapter 9

# Being Together is Very Good

"The difference in taking a nap alone with nobody at home and taking a nap when people are here at home is so easy to tell. Just notice the look on my face. When someone is here, I am reassured and secure. You cannot see me when I am alone, but I am sure my face is less relaxed and less calm. I am just better in so many ways when people are with me."

Rudy is well aware of how beneficial it is to be with one person or to be with several people. Rudy does not play alone. His toys are not moved when he is alone. When someone is at home, Rudy will eagerly get the toy and invite participation in play.

Rudy always has the skill and the ability to play. Those skills and abilities await a playmate. He cannot fetch the ball with total joy until someone throws it. He cannot pull harder on a towel in tug-of-war unless someone else also pulls.

Being together makes real, physical, tangible, visual, certain, manifested and experienced what alone remains stuck in the category of potential.

When Rudy and I walk, I always smile and I always laugh. If I walked the same steps alone there would be few, if any, smiles or laughs.

Rudy's vibrant sprinting, Rudy's intense investigation of a plant and its lovely aroma, Rudy's excitement when he sees another dog, these all create my smiles and laughs. I was able to smile and to laugh, but those did not occur until Rudy created a reason.

I am able to play although I rarely play anything. When Rudy brings the towel to me, he is inviting me to play, he is reminding me to play and he is inspiring me to play. Otherwise, I would not play.

For people whose life includes a dog like Rudy, there are benefits and blessings which otherwise life would not include. Dogs require much attention and care. Dogs need to be taken to the groomer or to the veterinarian. Dogs need to be fed. Dogs need toys. If the time, effort and expenses of having a dog were totaled, the sum would be significant. The cost is worth it.

Most of the life lessons from Rudy are based on how he lives and what his abundant living reveals about how to fully live. Life lesson nine comes more from how Rudy guides his family to live. Rudy brings out much good in the people who know him, who care for him, who care about him.

As Rudy fully lives, he helps the people who know him fully live. Rudy could have lived with another family in another place. He could have had a good life with that family at their home.

Yet in 2001, Bob, Laura, Robert, Julie and Brian decided to get a dog. They have given Rudy a very good life. Rudy has given as much or more.

Rudy has given joy, laughs, smiles, expressions of concern, company, love and an example of how to fully live. Rudy has required care which means his caregivers got to apply and to expand their ability to care. Rudy has expressed endless joy and love which means his family–a joyous and loving group of dear people–saw their joy and their love reciprocated.

How very life-affirming Rudy is. How convincingly Rudy reminds us that being together is very good.

Life Lesson Notes For The Reader:

Ways to apply Life Lesson 9–*Being Together is Very Good*:

In my life:

With family:

With friends:

At work or at school:

With other people or in other places:

# Chapter 10

# The Gospel According to Rudy

Rudy understands the Golden Rule and Rudy lives by the Golden Rule: "Do unto others as you would have them do unto you." (Matthew 7:12)

People like to be appreciated. People like to be loved. Rudy appreciates and loves people with every opportunity he is given plus with every opportunity he can create. His joy when family members return home is one example.

When Rudy celebrates with joy the return of a family member whether they were gone three hours, three days or some weeks, he is treating people the way people like to be treated and the way he likes to be treated. He hopes that his family will pay attention to him now that they are home, so he loves by example.

"You are home. I am so happy. We are together again. You

mean everything to me. You are precious to me. I am overjoyed to see you and to be with you."

Such a welcome is meaningful to anyone. Such a welcome would warm the heart of anyone. Rudy does not know the words of The Golden Rule. Rudy knows the meaning of The Golden Rule. Rudy lives by and exemplifies The Golden Rule.

Another important truth in The Gospel According to Rudy is "Love thy neighbor as thyself." (Matthew 22:39). Rudy never grows weary of expressing love. He loves as he likes to be loved–continuously.

There are times when Laura is at home doing hours of work on a computer. Rudy sits at her feet during those hours. What is he thinking? "She is working so hard. The best help I can give is to share this time with her. I hope she feels the love and the support which my presence is sending to her. I could be somewhere else, but I am needed here."

It is similar to Rudy's habit of rarely eating alone. He could be alone for six hours and not touch his food dish. When a family member arrives at home, Rudy will eventually eat. He seems to think it is impolite to dine alone. Perhaps he borrows a version of the mannerly idea of waiting until everyone is served before anyone starts to eat. He would want people to include him in meals so he delays his meals until someone is with him. Of course, he knows they can and will get their own food, but loving other people as you love yourself includes sharing activities such as meals together.

The Gospel According to Rudy includes an idea from James 2:17 in the New Testament of the Christian Bible: "Faith without action is dead."

Rudy has faith in naps. He puts that faith into action by taking many naps.

Rudy has faith in the value of walking. He puts that faith into action whenever he is given the opportunity to take a walk.

Rudy has faith in his family. He puts that faith into action by his constant expressions of devotion, affection and love toward his family.

Rudy has faith in life. He puts that faith into action by fully investing his total effort into each interaction that comes his way. He puts this faith in life into action by energetically exiting his overnight sleeping cage each morning to lovingly greet his family as he expresses joy and thanks.

The Gospel According to Rudy fully applies the truth of John 10:10 when Jesus says, "I came that they might have life and have it abundantly." Rudy lives an abundant life, but not with an understanding that abundance means more as in more possessions.

There are dogs with much more plush and elaborate overnight sleeping furniture than Rudy has. That may be exactly what those dogs prefer. Rudy is abundantly content with a metal cage and two towels. There he sleeps soundly, peacefully, securely. The abundance he values is not in the cost of the bedding, but in the complete assurance he has that all is well, safe and tranquil.

In all he does, Rudy lives life with an abundance of joy, of curiosity, of energy, of hope, of faith and of love. Rudy has mastered living. Real living, full living, abundant living. Rudy lives abundantly right here, right now, every moment, especially when he is with the family he cherishes and with the family all of whose members cherish this amazing dog.

It may seem unusual to reflect upon theology in terms of how a dog lives. Jesus did speak occasionally of animals. He did refer to sheep and how they would respond to the voice of their true shepherd.

Rudy is not a theologian. Rudy cannot read Holy Scripture or anything else. Rudy does not attend church. Rudy lives theology, lives scripture, lives church without realizing it.

Essentially, Rudy lives a life of love. Rudy gives love and receives love. Such is the essence of the Gospel According to Rudy. Rudy's gospel understanding has a strong connection to an essential idea from the Gospel of Jesus Christ according to the New Testament of the Christian Bible: love. Still, there is no substitute for the Bible, so do read the authentic gospels according to Matthew, Mark, Luke and John and see how Rudy's emphasis on love matches up.

If there is ever a time where you struggle with faith or when you find it difficult to love, just look at Rudy. His life is one big belief in love and one big, continuous experience of love. Great living, Rudy. You are teaching us well. The life lessons you have mastered and exemplified are gems of wisdom. Thanks, buddy, you are the best dog in the world.

Of course, every other dog owner thinks that his or her dog is the best dog in the world. That is how it should be.

Life Lesson Notes For The Reader:

Ways to apply Life Lesson 10–*The Gospel According to Rudy*:

In my life:

With family:

With friends:

At work or at school:

With other people or in other places:

# About the Author

**Dr. Keen Babbage, Ed. D.**

Keen J. Babbage has 30 years of experience as a teacher and administrator in middle school, high school, college, and graduate school.

He is the author of *911: The School Administrator's Guide to Crisis Management* (1996), *Meetings for School-Based Decision Making* (1997), *High- Impact Teaching: Overcoming Student Apathy* (1998), *Extreme Teaching* (2002), *Extreme Learning* (2004), *Extreme Students* (2005), *Results-Driven Teaching: Teach So Well That Every Student Learns* (2006), *Extreme Economics* (2007, 2009), *What Only Teachers Know about Education* (2008), *Extreme Writing* (2010), *The Extreme Principle* (2010), *The Dream and Reality of Teaching* (2011), *Reform Doesn't Work* (2012), *The Power of Middle School* (2012), *Teachers Know What Works: Actions That Experience Confirms Will Work* (2013), *Life Lessons From Cancer* (2013) and *Can Schools Survive?* (2014).

# Give Back to Markey

Keen's battle with cancer is documented in his terrific book, *Life Lessons from Cancer*. You can see what an important role the University of Kentucky Markey Cancer Center played in Keen's life and why he is so grateful to Markey. And to Rudy, his faithful companion.

The battle against cancer rages on, but you can play your part in fighting back by contributing to the great work occurring at the Markey Cancer Foundation through a monetary donation.

Cancer is not a temporary battle, it's a forever war, but as Dr. Babbage noted, all that matters is that we fight, fight more and keep fighting. Donate today.

To learn more about how you can help, visit
**http://www.markeycancerfoundation.org/fundraising.html**

# More Great
# Books from

**INTERNATIONAL RRP PUBLISHING & DIGITAL MEDIA**

Life Lessons from CANCER

Dr. Keen Babbage and Laura Babbage

With foreword by Don McNay

Learn more at:
**http://www.rrpinternational.org/#!life-lessons-from-cancer/cwh6**

Life Lessons from the
LOTTERY

Protecting Your Money in a Scary World

Don McNay CLU, ChFC, MSFS, CSSC

Author of best-selling books *Son of a Son of a Gambler:
Winners, Losers and What to Do When You Win the Lottery*
and *Wealth Without Wall Street*

Learn more at:
**http://www.rrpinternational.org/#!life-
lessons-from-the-lottery/c20vg**

Learn more at:
http://www.rrpinternational.org/#!don-
mcnays-greatest-hits/csza

Learn more at:
**http://www.rrpinternational.org/#!death-
by-lottery/c22rf**

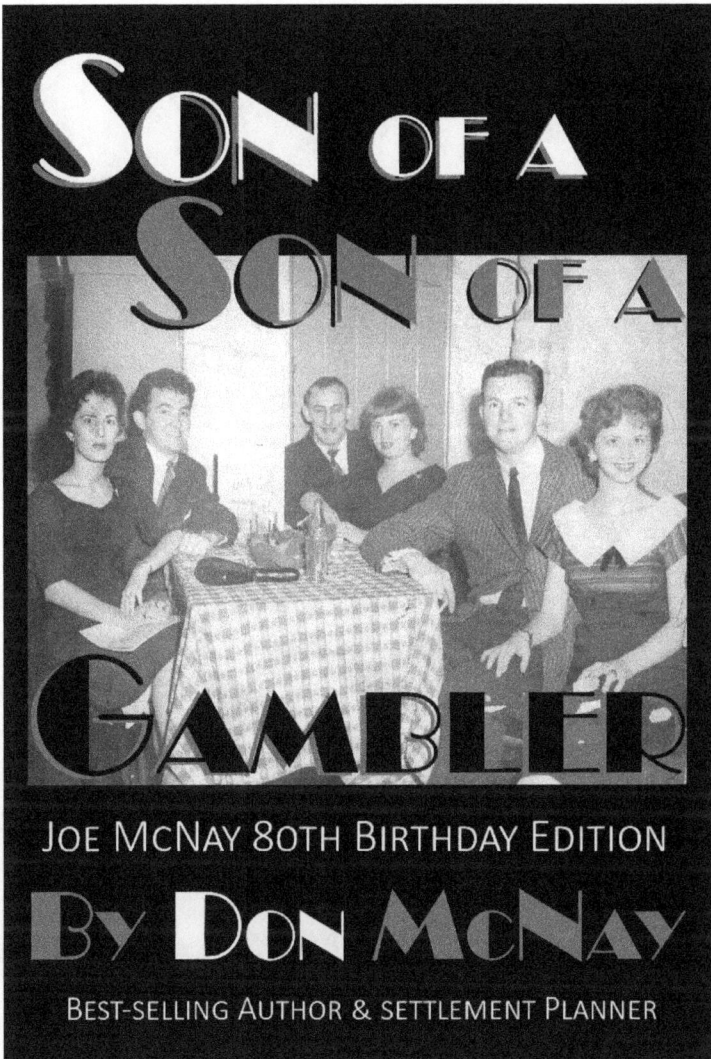

SON OF A SON OF A GAMBLER

JOE MCNAY 80TH BIRTHDAY EDITION

BY DON MCNAY

BEST-SELLING AUTHOR & SETTLEMENT PLANNER

Learn more at:
**http://www.rrpinternational.org/#!son-of-a-son-of-a-gambler-2/c15af**

Learn more at:
**http://www.rrpinternational.org/#!wealth-without-wall-street/cnz2**

Life Lessons from the
GOLF COURSE
The Quest for Spiritual Meaning,
Psychological Understanding and
Inner Peace through the Game of Golf

Clay Hamrick
PGA PROFESSIONAL

With Don McNay CLU, ChFC, MSFS, CSSC
Best-selling author of *Life Lessons from the Lottery:
Protecting Your Money in a Scary World*

Learn more at:
**http://www.rrpinternational.org/#!life-
lessons-from-the-golf-cou/cz4z**

The Art of
Opinion Writing

Dave Astor Robert C. Koehler Joel Brinkley
Michael R. Masterson Clarence Page Kathleen Parker Mark Hopkins
Cal Thomas Lynne Varner Joanna Weiss Connie Schultz Jeffrey L. Seglin
Derrick Z. Jackson Dave Lieber Ellen Goodman

Insider Secrets from Top Op-Ed Columnists

Suzette Martinez Standring

Learn more at:
**http://www.rrpinternational.org/#!the-art-
of-opinion-writing/cp3z**

The
Art of
Column
Writing

Insider Secrets from Art Buchwald, Dave Barry, Arianna Huffington, Pete Hamill and Other Great Columnists

Suzette Martinez Standring

Learn more at:
http://www.rrpinternational.org/#!the-art-of-column-writing/c12oi

**INTERNATIONAL RRP DIGITAL MEDIA**

We are experts in creating web sites and providing a social media experience for businesses, attorneys, and political campaigns.

Check out some of our previous sites:

**www.lotteryguru.org**

**www.donmcnay.com**

**www.attorneyfees.org**

**www.conservators.info**

For more information, visit our contact page to get in touch directly with Adam Turner, Editorial Director of RRP International at **aturner@rrpinternational.org** or (859) 429-1782.

**www.rrpinternational.org**